The Mind is a Timeless Machine

– V. Nova

Artificial Intelligence

Versus

Living Mind Intelligence

V. NOVA

ISBN: 978-1-80623-159-1 eBook

978-1-80623-160-7 Paperback

978-1-80623-178-2 Hardcover

Printed in the United States of America

From the pioneering educational series of the new publications reflecting the recent research and findings on the human mind and its inborn mechanism of the perceptions of realities

CONTENTS

PREFACE

V. Nova is an American writer, a lifelong independent cross-disciplinary researcher, an innovative artist, and a contemporary philosopher.

"Artificial Intelligence Versus Living Intelligence" is the first educational publication from the series of books suggesting a comprehensive revision of the extant knowledge that we are taught in schools and learn from the daily news/media.

A popular understanding of artificial intelligence (AI) and the related rapid development of mass production in contemporary industries is missing a comprehensive revision, based on higher knowledge, experience and understanding on whether it can be considered as true progress in society.

If you expect V. Nova's thoughts in this publication to be identical to the popular concepts and beliefs regarding technological progress, you would be mistaken. However, you would not be disappointed while reading the notes on Nova's unconventional research approach.

I had a few discussions with the author before I wrote this Preface.

Nova has been working on this new series of educational books for many years. Traditional education is mainly focused on training us in mimicking the established patterns of socializing, thinking, and working by following the rules of the communities where we live. This type of conventional education that we traditionally receive presumably helps us socialize using our traditional language, basic knowledge in mathematics, popular morals, and communication. We believe that it would enable us to get along with the rest of society.

However, it can be challenging for some individuals to adapt to these norms, as it is not natural for individuals as newborns to follow social patterns. Society creates social systems and rules under its artificially established orders that are not meant to serve a real person but rather a non-existent collective human prototype that can follow such artificially established rules. Some individuals or groups just break or avoid the conventional rules for a good or no intelligent reason, and some become completely psychologically disoriented, and eventually suffer a mental disorientation or indigestion of experience, or what we call a mental impairment.

Nova explains that we are overlooking the deeply penetrating conditions that we inevitably experience and are getting affected by them every moment of our lives.

It appears as though we are becoming excited while observing and playing with the visible stages of the theatrical and amusingly pictorial human consciousness of our minds: the place in the mind where our unique realities reside but remain incomprehensible to this very day. Nova points out how we are uninterested in the types of invisible universal powers that are driving all the objects, spectacles, and characters in their endless actions and interactions on the stages of our observations. "This is not the objective world out there that we might see as we think. The mighty world cannot fit our human visions, and no one can fly out of one's own mind to observe the world objectively. The grand reason why we see only the internally processed stages of our own internal minds is that if we could jump out, we may not remain selves even for an instant, crushed in the colossal powers of flux. The observer is our mind, which also creates and builds its internal realities with great limitations. Limitations work for a mind as sculptor's chisels carving out our realities. A mind is creating its matter from ever-changing sensations, we only randomly perceive from our fluctuating environments."

"In the following chapters, we revise our current and still poor mentality based on our contemporary visions of the Cosmos and ourselves observing it. This is the very mentality that is primarily driving our current mass thinking, excitement and activities into pictorial illusions of the nonexistence."

In this book, V. Nova suggests that it is important for us to seek explanations for the questions that we all ask in our minds, particularly the subconscious mind.

One of them is as follows: while we witness considerable progress in the technological development in our society, why is the development and evolvement in our social life, minds, and bodies impeded? “We still cannot understand each other any better than millennia ago.”

A pertinent question is that despite using innumerable gadgets to stay connected with each other we continue to create conflicts, fight and wage wars. Nova explains this situation as follows: “Contemporary scientists unlike independent scientists of the past are paid by the industries and political rulers for primarily serving some highly questionable ideas and develop innovative technologies to promote illusion of questionable in true values discoveries and “progress”. What we call AI, and mass production of all sorts of communication gadgets and systems to sell to excited masses, who are "learning" to only punch some buttons and keys, no progress in human true knowledge and intelligence but troubling behaviors of masses have been recently admitted."

Human knowledge and intelligence have not developed any further than the point where we keep primitively mimicking nature's creative ways and failing to learn about mutual coexistence with nature. It is profitable to produce and sell technology to the masses to replace manual tasks and tasks that require cognitive skills. Advanced technologies are now advertising ambiguous messages about the superiority of AI that can replace our poor knowledge and low mental capacities. Nova elucidates this phenomenon as follows: "Artificial technology cannot compensate for great human ignorance, as technology cannot really think, neither on its own nor for our living minds."

In this presentation, I have decided to use Nova's words to the extent possible to present her pioneering observations and innovative thinking. This task was highly challenging, as Nova's expressions are her original vision of an independent, unorthodox researcher offering her valuable insight into the nature of the human mind.

The experience that our institutions have collected today is missing a solid foundation.

Since ancient times, only a few milestones have been achieved in the future foundation of human thought.

However, it is forgotten as a material for studying and building new thoughts in every field. The Greek philosopher Heraclitus's teachings on flux and the profound thoughts of the great Greek philosopher Protagoras on unavoidable limitations remain as the rare notes and partial citations in a hostile piece written by Plato against the magnificent work of great Greek philosophers and Plato's contemporaries.

Despite all the challenges, these extremely rare notes of the great philosophers of antiquity have miraculously survived for several millennia.

Nova believes in the survival of the bright minds who are keen to learn independently, away from the rigidity of established institutions and are able to pick up from where the great philosophers in history left off. From the wisdom of the past, we are invited to discover a new future. V. Nova, a cross-disciplinary researcher, shares her new findings from the under-researched field of the nature of the human mind. Nova invites curious readers of all ages and interests to explore this path.

When do we begin learning? Perhaps since the day that we are born, and since the time that we feel a certain unstoppable vibration-like metamorphosis within ourselves. This reveals that our tiny newborn bodies *existed* as long as we could sense them. When we sense something, we inevitably experience change that is invisible energy actually empowering our living minds. We can already subconsciously *feel* the millennia-old wisdom articulated by the great philosopher Heraclitus: "No man can step in the same river twice, as the river is not the same river, and the man is not the same man."

This immortal philosophical quote by Heraclitus remains the most fundamental discovery on the true nature of the world. This teaching would enable even the most youthful mind to recognize its true self before it gets caught up in some generic name or number (age) related to what we mistakenly believe is the true identity of a person. Everyone has their unique identity within their mind.

In all its transformations, flux is a fundamental concept that offers an explanation on why even the smallest event in world existence is completely unique. The perfect ideals are primitive products of our human imagination.

"No real balance, exact equality, equity, identical copies of anything, repetitions, symmetry, conservation of energy, perfect reversal, or absolute isolation is ever possible under the colossal power of Flux." This fundamental concept proposed by Nova can facilitate the development of a new institution.

Nova explains that we observe *sameness* and repetition because human perception, particularly through our poorly developed human bodily organs, is rather *crude, and our naked eye cannot notice instances of the minuscule changes in nature.* This condition of the human *crudeness* of perceptions needs to be considered in learning, teaching, and innovation, and in the development of social, industrial, and technological structures.

Human minds do not need gasoline or nuclear energy. To truly evolve, we must reclaim nature's creative powers within our living minds and temporary physical bodies. Our invisible primary sensations are constantly interacting with the mighty world. The mental energies that we produce are within the scope of perceptual sensing. Therefore, these sensations are transformed through the perception of our mind into our visions and imaginations, memories, and thinking. However, this is not a mechanical process but rather an ongoing, evolving act.

We are born without any dependence on artificial machines or systems.

All varieties of living existence have tremendous potential to sense the transforming environments, including the visible and the invisible.

We all can easily feel that the world that we sense around us is constantly changing. Therefore, our sensations, feelings, imagination, memory, and thinking are also transforming. This metamorphic existence is immensely powerful while simultaneously gentle and vital, and it can change us in the blink of an eye. Despite technological advancements, no artificially produced systems can match the powers and endless novelty in nature. Why not create small systems that are easier to maintain, fix, improve, or even replace if needed, without provoking colossal global disasters as huge systems sooner or later but unavoidably "create?"

One may wonder: why do human beings, unlike other living creatures, feel the desperate need for artificially created tools, food, clothing, and entertainment? Why do we forcefully alter the natural environment by trying to fix everything that we do not like or understand? We often deny the very existence of something that we cannot accept, calculate, or measure.

Human beings are different from other life on this planet. We mimic nature in countless ways, whether for survival or entertainment. We marvel at the effortless flight of the birds, admire the living beings in the deep oceans, and watch the unrestrained grace and keen instincts of wild creatures, such as the big cats and deer.

Despite our considerable efforts to mimic nature and our desires to have skills similar to the most gifted survivors in the wilderness on Earth, we remain dependent on our crude, man-made artificial devices. We clothe our vulnerable bodies to protect ourselves from the elements, and we build heavy, noisy machines/devices in our attempts to fly or dive in water—feats that can never be as true and natural as the actions of the birds, insects, or living beings in the ocean. Our human creations are impressive only in our eyes and are actually crude and perhaps caricaturish imitations of the magnificent, graceful, meaningful, and efficient designs in nature. **Nova describes our questionable progress in creating technology and AI as the industries producing crutches for human beings as physical and mental invalids.**

Why are we so reliant on artificial systems? Why do we construct elaborate economic models and systems that so often fail to function as intended, falling under the unpredictable forces of nature?

After all, Is it possible that what we perceive as imperfections in nature may, in reality, be nature's unyielding call for adaptation and improvement within ourselves?

As V. Nova writes in this pioneering educational series, "We can change ourselves and begin to naturally evolve ourselves by learning to coexist with each other and natural laws. We cannot evolve our living minds and bodies by inventing more and more A.I. and other mental and physical crutches on which we keep depending on, avoiding much comprehension about how our manmade toys we constantly play effect our own nature. First, we must discover *how our own minds work and produce their own energies that heal our own natura. Moreover, the living mind is impossible to unplug.*"

This research seeks to examine the root of the instinctive behavior of the human mind, its creative perceptions, and the unrecognized before interactive nature's forces that help us shape what we experience as our reality.

At the core of our life experiences, we learn that our internal driving "mechanism" lies within the mind's extraordinary ability to perceive or sense, see, hear, smell, and feel. Nova invites us to uncover aspects that are invisible to our physical bodies, which enable our mind to eventually form visible impressions from the instinctive and instantly fluctuating sensations within our environments.

Why is it that the living mind, unlike artificial systems, cannot be simply "unplugged?" The reason is that the human mind possesses its own power.

These questions and answers are central to our understanding of the nature of a living mind, whose ephemeral functions and power cannot be controlled by artificial "chips." A physical brain is not a creative mind but one of the bodily organs, working as a transmitter.

Whether we are awake, asleep, dreaming, fantasizing, or thinking, our mind is constantly working toward organizing and interpreting the sensory input that it constantly receives. This process is not confined to artists or those trained in the creative fields; it is an instinctive living mechanism of the perceptions of the human mind. Nova's pioneering work explains the process of how each mind continuously *compares, selects, composes, focuses on something that attracts it, and frames* its random sensations, shaping a unique reality and its impressions that we may eventually observe. What we experience is not the world "as it is," but rather, we live by producing the visions while creating these from our sensations and feelings. Our minds interpret their unique primary sensations, which are not identical to those of others. A mind gradually pieces together these impressions, but for only moments, and composes them in similar but always slightly different ways.

Every mind takes its own time to process its unique realities. We are behind the timing of worldly existence in that we believe that we should imaginably remain fixated on something that is "out there." There is nothing "fixed" in the unstoppable existence of flux. Even bodily sensations, such as pain or joy, must first be processed by the mind before we become aware of them—a process that requires time and interpretation, while the mighty world is constantly transforming into different new worlds that we are unaware of.

While these research findings are novel, they are subconsciously related to each individual. We begin developing wisdom from where the most deeply intuitive philosophical thinkers, such as Heraclitus and Protagoras, the great logician George Berkeley, and the contemporary philosopher and physicist Werner Heisenberg, left off.

Is real distance possible in an existence that is constantly undergoing interactive transformations? Nova repeatedly enquires: “How do we explain our crudely primitive idea of ‘distance’ when one sees the sun is up greatly away in the cosmos and ‘untouchable’, but one’s skin gets burnt rather quickly? We may feel distances only through nature’s elements “around” us that change within ourselves.”

Nova suggests that the answers to this question are based on the fundamental laws of the world and not some confusing responses found through complicated computing. Heisenberg revealed that if one wishes to become a true scientist, one must first become an independent learning–thinking philosopher. True scientists are aware that when we open our eyes, they do not reveal the world as it is.

Contemporary sciences primarily serve innovative technologies. Scientists are fantasizing. Technology becomes highly profitable when it is mass-produced for selling products and making profits. At present, technologies advertise through loud but confusing messaging about AI tools that are prevailing and can replace our poor mental capacities. Nova explains that artificial technology cannot replace great human ignorance as advertised, as AI tools cannot independently process thoughts.

Despite this perceptional adaptability that is naturally granted to us from birth, we ignore our inborn talents, as the process of thinking helps us recognize these abilities of perception within oneself as God's vital blessing for the creativity and wisdom required for survival.

Why are we becoming increasingly dependent on artificial technologies that are making human minds lazy and less active?

We continue to remain ignorant of our potentially remarkable abilities as living beings. We are gradually beginning to realize that the brain does not think or the eyes do not see—only a sovereign creative mind does.

No researcher has ever scanned an image of our reality, thoughts, or dreams within the physical structure of the brain. The mind's creative and interpretive processes are extremely intimate, personal, and unique and cannot be copied, replicated, or controlled and reduced to mere mechanical operations.

As we become increasingly reliant on technology, we must ask ourselves if we are truly advancing or merely compensating for our inability or slowness to naturally adapt to our ever-changing environments.

In today's world, people rely on their devices for even the simplest tasks—navigating their surroundings, checking the weather, and accessing in all sorts of information. Without these manmade gadgets and tools, transportation and artificially manufactured items, including fast food, many feel lost and helpless, resembling invalids who cannot function without their crutches. Is this dependence a sign of progress, or does it signal a warning about a deeper regression in our mental and physical capabilities?

An adult mind must recognize that birds fly using the wings that they have naturally grown. When a human being is confined within a noisy, vibrating, artificially constructed capsule, it restricts their ability to fly.

As technology advances, we must critically question whether it is enhancing our human intelligence or diminishing our undiscovered natural abilities to evolve. Are we able to exist and live as discerning human beings?

Moreover, the sickly individuals abuse the technology advances to easily destroy anything they would not reach without abusing technology. Technology cannot choose in cases whether it shall help or demolish. "Artificial technology cannot replace great human ignorance as advertised, as AI tools cannot independently process thoughts".

If we learn to understand the natural abilities of our mind and its powerful vitality as our endless source of life, we may begin to see the world, and ourselves in it, from a new perspective.

S. Waterhouse

INTRODUCTION

As we become increasingly reliant on technology, we must ask ourselves if we are truly advancing or merely compensating for our inability and slowness to naturally adapt to our ever-changing environments. Let's take a look at ourselves as we are well equipped with all the new advanced gadgets in our pockets, personal transportation, clothes and processed food, medications and highly questionable knowledge about "the world" from news practically replacing our own thinking.

Are we, human beings, who are becoming the masters of the universe?

Or are we still undeveloped human beings who are still unable to evolve, and therefore, increasingly feel the need to produce all sorts of tools that can artificially help our poor human sight, sense of smell, hearing and still clumsy from birth physical bodies somehow succeed and become more sufficient? Are AI technology and other artificial crutches truly compensating for our human vulnerabilities while simultaneously reinforcing our dependence on external artificial aids?

Artificial intelligence, digital communication, or mechanical devices do not manifest true human intelligence. Rather, they surprisingly highlight the great limitations of our undeveloped and poor physical and mental capacities.

Can we answer: what is the difference between an ephemeral mind and a physical brain? Why is that no researcher, surgeon or a butcher can find any image, thought or pictures of our reality in brains?

To find the true answer to these questions, is a necessity for our human survival. As of today, we are only familiar with confusing explanations suffering illogical and superficial observations.

The believers in Creator easily accept that a mind is an entity of a living soul or a spirit. It is so far written: “What no eye has seen, what no ear has heard, and what no human mind has conceived" "these are the things God can revealed to us only by his Spirit."

However, it is not a usual explanation found in scientific fields.

The pioneering contemporary research reflected in this book suggests the advanced learning about a mind existence that is granted by nature with a "Mechanism of perception" that is revealing our natural abilities to evolve our minds and possibly physical bodies.

Can your brain become a scientific model of a robot, built from manmade parts, manipulated, plugged in, or disconnected, killed by elements such as fire or in the total absence of artificial power that is needed for running this very robot-mind?

Or you are living on energies that your mind/sprit instinctively produces on its own, just from unstoppable interactions with the mighty world and its transformations?

CHAPTER 1

There are no stars out there, no trees or water.

The world we are made of is a *Flux* that exists for less than an instant, entirely new, with all its births and deaths. At its deep core, every living being keeps interacting with invisible instances of ever-changing conditions of nature. Nature is unstoppable change. If the worlds of all existences are about instant transformations and therefore entirely metamorphic in their deepest stage, *how* can not just we but any sort of living being survive in this endless whirlpool of ever-new, unrepeatable nature?

Although our human bodily sensory organs are still poorly developed and no technologies can even remotely compensate for our physical inability to survive and evolve wisely, our pride and sense of superiority over other forms of existence only boldly reveal our weaknesses and unnecessary struggles compared to other forms of self-evolving life using neither artificial gadgets nor energies.

If we grasp the following further on in these writing observations, we could discover and possibly comprehend the precious gifts of nature that we human beings unintentionally bury behind the visible spectacles of the superficial consciousness of our playful minds, where they remain unnoticed to this day.

We still remain unaware of the endless instances of change that affect our entire existence as the deepest driving force of life.

What abilities are we as living beings granted by nature just to *be*? For the first time, we are about to recognize and describe this quintessential gift granted to us from birth as *nature's mechanism of perception*.

Our *perceiving* is a *process* revealing our absolute inability to "reflect" anything as it is "out there." It is the most creatively vital process of life at its very core.

It is not possible even for any snowflake to be identical to another, as in the world of minuscule ever-new instants our entire existence is never identically and perfectly the same.

How can the Self be able to recognize itself in this Flux? Previous attempts to answer this question have been made solely through convenient references to the mighty Creator's own power and will. Although it is rather absurd to think that the Creator would channel his infinite inspiration to create the ultimately silly mess we make of our lives, and how we choose to excuse ourselves for our self-inflicted troubles and avoid true learning, wondering, and thinking any further on for ourselves. However, our weaknesses teach us something grand about our existence as human beings.

Since prehistoric times, we have attempted to "reproduce" the design of nature as a model at the level of human interpretation. Specifically, based on our highly limited perception of physical sight, we continue to serve our observations of what we call "the world" and even construct the "perfect" order of "things" around us to explain for ourselves our constantly challenging experiences of all kinds.

As we begin and continue recognizing our abilities through our vision, based on what we see through physical sensory organs, we discover how limited, illusive, and deceiving our impressions of human reality are. We realize that by fashioning our models based on what mother nature creates, we simply produce caricatured man- made machines, only mimicking mighty nature while missing out on its creative abilities within timelessly unstoppable and unpredictable Flux. We express what we feel and see in our specific ways as human beings through the sciences, poetry, arts, music, and philosophy. However, we curiously ignore something in our picturesque and playful mental theater of consciousness: the powers that are igniting, animating, and turning absolutely invisible in their natural instances of change into spectacles that we may eventually observe. There is no way to stop the worlds of Flux, even in our observations. We cannot ever sense or know beyond what we are.

The ancient Greek sage Heraclitus described this fundamental condition of universal existence as Flux. Observations, knowledge, or any impressions of our human experience do not exist on their own “out there,” and nothing can be “reflected from out there” as it is. What we call “perceiving” is the only possible way to interact with and sense the world around us. Thus we are to digest information we perceive, revealing for ourselves a vital process of life under the powers of the fundamental laws of irreversible instant change. The old musician once said to a young one who was scared of his mistake while rehearsing with a Jazz band: We do not make mistakes - it is Jazz. Transformations of Flux allow our unique living beings not only to somehow interact within “outer” existences of myriad worlds but eventually randomly feel our primary interactions within and without, moreover, instinctively we transform ourselves into different selves, along with our primary and invisible sensations that are creating new unique visions, observations, knowledge, and experience.

Every living mind has its own creative abilities for the sake of its very existence and its continuity. My humble message for a believer is that God grants you your blessed freedom to choose to create your own realities within all the abundance and challenges of the worlds while learning from your spiritual parent to create, thus discovering the wisdom of endless vitality.

Since early childhood, we all intuitively sense metamorphic instances of what we instinctively feel as vibrations or transformations within ourselves; however, we begin to ignore this deeply intuitive sensation of unavoidable instability as we grow up. In human society, we choose not to notice the greatest power of Flux, which the sage of antiquity, Heraclitus, described as the most colossal and unavoidable condition of the world. This fundamental condition is the source of all conditions in the entirety of our everyday experiences, calculations, and experiments, and, moreover, in our modeling of all types of man-made structures that we presumably imagine to represent reality, may or shall be crudely simplified to satisfy our deduced understanding and judgment.

I invite my curious reader—and I hope to find one or two—to discover *how* the very creation of visions of what we see as the Earth reality embraced by the universe occurs not "out there" but within each unique mind. We simply can not fly out our own minds to see anything beyond what we are.

The mind's production can be expressed in myriad ways based on our observations as human beings, but our expressions cannot reflect even the tiniest fragment of the mighty world as it is. How can we ever manage to do that if the magnificent world of Flux cannot repeat any of its unique instants? The instants of the endless metamorphoses of the world have no time or space to keep handy for us to measure our ideas of time and space.

The question of why the entire existence of the instantly new myriad worlds of which we are unaware has such an ephemeral nature remains unanswered in our existing collective knowledge. In our age of some revealing scientific experiments regarding ephemeral nature of what we, humans, somehow sense as "matter" we meet primitive in learning "materialists" reducing nature to the degree of our technical measurements that cannot perfectly preserve exactly the same conditions of reality even for an instant. However, our sense of bodily reality is still so crude that it is handy for us to apply some measurements.

In the following chapters, the first step toward an independent search as to *how* in the first place we *are able* to exist as sovereign selves and uniquely sense, observe, memorize, and think in this world of endless, instantly appearing, and disappearing metamorphic existences.

What kinds of abilities are we granted by God's nature of the magnificent Flux to be able to live as individual beings without completely melting down into forever new and unique instants of the endlessly ephemeral worlds of unstoppable change?

I believe that these primary abilities in life are unavoidably and authentically creative or artistic and serve a much greater purpose than what is usually understood as creativity in the arts. These internal primary abilities allow every living being to *be*, while surviving and evolving as a more or less unique individual, along with the unique circumstances of endless change. Having these inborn abilities makes it easy for us to discover and begin to comprehend by watching the process of how we perceive what we believe reality is.

We are unable even to sense anything unless the inborn living *mechanism of perception* in our minds is "at work," transforming our primary and yet invisible instances of interactions into our unique internal compositions of realities that we observe as playhouses within our minds. How does this creative mechanism function and reveal itself?

Any living mind is a little creator of a unique self, as it can intuitively reproduce itself through changing within entirely and ceaselessly transforming environments.

Whether gifted or not, we never exist as exactly the same identical units, as it would be impossible for us—unique beings—to face and sense exactly repetitive conditions, as these are impossible anywhere. Therefore, we cannot have exactly the same experiences, knowledge, or ideas. We are able to create new selves as long as we are alive. We are amazingly free to learn and live through intimate, unique, and ever-changing experiences, whether all that may seem to us is more or less "the same."

How do we recognize memories, things an events as "the same." The most fundamental reasons for our existence are within ourselves, but we often fail to find them. Anyone can discover the essence of oneself, and this adventure is what we here embark on, forming the basis of this study and described in the following notes.

Why is it that nothing and no one can be treated in the exact same way as our societies, politicians, industrialists, and medical professionals often insist on, for the sake of serving the same rigid manmade rules and laws by crudely adjusting living beings to non-existing dull collective prototypes impossible in the living world?

Every single life is blessed from its birth with the primordial freedom to be its unique Self, created within its internal and sovereign mind's residence.

No real balance, exact equality, equity, identical copies of anything, repetitions, symmetry, perfect reversal, conservation of mass or anything else, or absolute isolation is ever possible under the colossal powers of Flux. Every life entity is unique within itself, as this is the only way to exist as a single self, as well as facilitate the existence of many selves. Absolute copies would absorb one another and cease to exist under the mighty powers of Flux. In our worlds of instant metamorphosis, we are always dealing with—in ways more or less practical for us—*approximations of our experiences*, never with any sort of exactness other than in our imagination. Why is it that our perceptions are forever crude, and therefore, we all imagine "the same thing"?

While reading the first chapter of this work, one can easily discover the crucially vital nature of the very process of perceiving conditions ignited by Flux within oneself—and how under these conditions we build our experiences and knowledge, but only from what we are able to perceive and compose.

To absolutely know *something*, we must entirely become this very *something*, losing the uniqueness of our original selves.

CHAPTER 2

We have a wonderful ability to *Compare* our perceptions with our previous experiences. No life is possible without the ability to *Compare* sensations. The primitive visions that we depict, observe, analyze, calculate, and prove or disprove are based on strictly limited human corporeal perceptions, which we somehow may record and collect as impressions. Even our impressions cannot be frozen and stay perfectly unchanged even for a moment, though we may not notice any changes for a while. The training in our education systems and established systematic methods of obtaining knowledge curiously demonstrate and characterize rather rigid habits to be followed in patterns of thinking, rather than a true vital assimilation of experiences. The habit of following patterns is often called professionalism. This can work and even be helpful in some cases unless our ever-changing environments surprise us with the unexpected tasks.

We cannot avoid our very process of perceiving as a continuous, exclusively internal mental process. The "things" or events are invisible to us until they are uniquely turned in each of our minds into more or less unique mental productions. However, nothing produced in our minds can be visible or sensed outside our minds as these visions have been originally and internally produced.

We communicate by expressing our experiences while creating and symbolically assembling our collectively rendered images, sounds, language, opinions, and prototypes based on our presumably similar experiences. This is how we mistake our collective opinions and symbolic images for "objective" reality, and commonly use these to prove an "objective" truth and even knowledge.

Can objective reality that is "out there" fit in our minds as it is?

The "tangible" or physical realities we may sense are not "objective," not "out there," as they are impossible on their own unless we process our own primary non-physical sensations into uniquely tangible and even visible subjects in each of our minds. The playful appearances of impressions we perceive through the unique bodily organs called eyes, or what we term sight, have been extensively researched and described as shallow and deceiving. Sifted through the bodily organs these appearances are made possible, but they are not inside the physical bodily organs. The perceiver and producer of visions are our ephemeral minds, responsible for processing our unique momentary sensations into thoughts, feelings, and appearances. Sadly, the possible explanations for these illusive visions formed in our minds we commonly mistake for objective reality.

Truly convincing explanations of this phenomenon have been missing in our history of research and, to this day, in the entirety of the contemporary sciences. How does this occur?

To explain the illusiveness of our sight, on which we rely our knowledge, one must finally dare to ask, *How* in the first place does all of what we see and analyze get into our own minds? Why is it that no images or thoughts can be found in any of the physical organs especially the brain? **The bodily organs cannot observe or think on their own.**

Where is the mind "located," the thinking, memorizing, dreaming, fantasizing, sensing, and feeling mind, which moreover *observes* objects and events, brains and bodies, other living beings, or universal landscapes?

We now begin to enter the unknown field of our mind to discover ourselves in it while bringing our learning further along from where the great sages and philosophers of ancient Greece left off.

Although deeply intuitive philosophers in our history have contemplated and articulated the impossibility of us reflecting anything as it is "out there," such notions have not been explained and are highly inconvenient for us to even admit and to accept in our contemporary schools of learning.

Despite observing and experiencing our manmade staged theater of societies, constituting habits, rules, and orders that we try to follow with great difficulty, we naively believe that we live in an open world.

As we begin to discover for ourselves, and within ourselves, the most magnificent fundamental natural law of *Flux*, and our inborn abilities to perceive our unique realities, the confounding human notion of "reflecting" reality "out there," especially within our brains, would prove absolutely futile.

Can we furnish a physical organ, called the brain, with objects as they are out there?

Again, *how* is it possible for us to perceive and observe memories and think, imagine, and feel some *differences* in what we observe? We are about to discover our *perceptions,* not as mirror-like flattish reflections imprinted on our brains, but as the most vivid of nature's tools for sensing and *processing* our lives within ourselves.

We may see similarities in thinking between the contemporary sciences and the lovely and well-known expressions in the arts and poetry, such as William Blake's poetry, where he describes our eyes as "open windows" to the world. Another poetical quote by Blake sounds as contemporary as scientific beliefs regarding future technologies: "If the doors of perception were cleansed, everything would appear to man as it is infinite" (featured in the work *The Marriage of Heaven and Hell* by the English poet and printmaker William Blake).

However, Marcel Proust suggested, somewhat more daringly, *"The real voyage of discovery consists, not in seeking new landscapes, but in having new eyes."* "La Prisonnière," the fifth volume of "Remembrance of Things Past" (also known as) "In Search of Lost Time."

Nonetheless, how can a mind sense and perceive visions on its own when using no physical eyes, ears, brain, or any other corporeal sensory organs of a body in dreams, thinking, or imagining?

I would further encourage you to understand Proust's "new eyes" metaphorically, as a suggestion to find a new, even drastically different perception of not physical eyes but the mind's eye contemplating its internal mental existence.

Therefore, we seek a new field of experience. We have more precious undiscovered findings ahead—our as-yet unappreciated gifts of nature for life. I suggest the pursuit of unconventional research beginning from the most vital functions of our mind driven by nature's vital *mechanism of perceptions.*

I would not be surprised to face conventional criticism resting on the same old-fashioned and stubbornly rigid patterns of thinking, habits, and behavior that are misleading our society to remain unaware of the mighty laws of nature that seemingly no one is able to circumvent. The permanently immeasurable and absolutely untouchable powers of *Flux* crush this human ignorance. Restrictiveness in the sciences that we are taught leaves new findings of all types that are poorly explained and are only sorted out by labeled categories. Within established patterns of thinking, the possibility of fundamental discoveries to find new solutions to solve our problems would never be possible.

CHAPTER 3

Can we ever hope to evolve as authentically creative species in the amazing conditions of ephemeral Flux? Pursuing our still-primitive human desires to capture, use, and abuse everything we think is possible to reach, to "know" by mindlessly manipulating, fixing, or destroying the unknown life for the sake of artificial temporary conveniences, comforts, and fashions, we have built thick walls of "progress" blocking us from wisely learning about coexistence within natural environments that are ever new to us, the only conditions where we may coherently evolve ourselves.

However, we are just a step or two away from discovering *how* to at least begin to creatively evolve. Where is a mind?

Our unique human minds interact with the ever-changing temporary vessels of our physical bodies, which are taking us on a journey that we call physical experience. By sensing these unique interactions, we can learn that the formations of living organisms are not truly "solid" entities, and we can see through the modest achievements in the sciences that bodies are combinations of living cells, atoms, viruses, bacteria, tissues, and other microscopic organisms that form bodily parts and sensory organs. We can also see that everything within the vessel of a body has its internal environment, and, as contemporary scientific knowledge states, ninety-nine percent of the human body is made up of carbon, hydrogen, nitrogen, and oxygen atoms, along with those of other chemical elements.

One might wonder, "Is this me? Who am I—cells, atoms, viruses in water? How can I be my Self surviving among so many different organisms composing a body that I strangely interact with and feel, but which I do not truthfully know at all?" Are these bodies things-in-themselves? How do we sense them?

Through such contemplations, one's deep intuition reveals that one possesses a Self, a living mind, a spirit, a soul, allowing one to be an entity and be able to willingly observe, think, memorize, and even more or less comprehend one's own existence. However, is it possible to explain *how* a bodyless *mind manages to sense on its own*, whether using a corporeal body or not, and above all, to exist creatively and sense itself without the eyes, ears, brain, or any other bodily sensory organs?

However, when temporary bodies are disconnected from sensations in the mind, they become paralyzed, fall apart, and die.

The new field of discovery is beyond the deceiving landscapes that we are observing at the stage of the mind's playful and constantly fluctuating theatrical spectacles. What we call consciousness is awaiting for our step, beyond its curtains. We observe our shallow spectacles of consciousness only as long as our minds intuitively sift our mental sensations while interacting through our bodily organs, especially in relation to sight.

CHAPTER 4

Taking a step beyond the thick curtains of the flattish consciousness of our mind might be quite a challenging adventure for us when we are ruled by our conventional thinking patterns.

In contemporary schools, before undergoing training in grammar and math, no student has the opportunity to acquire basic knowledge about *how we manage to see what we see. Why* is it that the physical organs called the eyes cannot actually see on their own?

The first explanation is that we observe some appearances, but only internally, after perceiving and processing invisible momentary sensations. We must perceive/process our sensations because we may never sense anything directly as it is "out there." We are limited. Our observing abilities rely on an internal mental process, which we are about to discover. Why these limitations though? Is this a curse or a protective gift from mother nature showing the reason for why we are unable to reflect our environments as it is and as we so wish, directly?

If one could miraculously fly outside of oneself just to see realities outside of oneself objectively, the colossal powers of Flux creating endlessly new transformations would melt one down, in no time, as a tiny lump of sugar in a hot cup of tea. Every living mind has its unique *limitations*, not just for challenging obstacles, but initially to serve every single life as great *protective boundaries*.

First, Newtonian or Einsteinian laws and conditions, or any other classical theories described in physics, chemistry, biology, or mathematics, are not universal natural laws. These conditions and our explanations following our physical laws only indicate our specific and limited human experience, which is mainly affected by our unique bodily sensations and our specific mental perceptions of these corporeal temporary sensations. These sensations of what we recognize as physical have been processed in our minds, but mainly come from our bodily sensory organs and their interactions in the limited, not objective, surrounding environments.

In other words, these physical impressions are based on conditions of our bodies, which we mistakenly imagine are providing reflections of "objective" reality through sensory abilities such as corporeal sight.

Ironically, the proof of these "realities" found through the sciences is mainly based upon recorded appearances perceived through this very corporeal sight, which is known in the field of psychology of human perception to be the most deceptive, illusive, tricky, and superficial sensory perception of all those we may possess. The sciences must thoroughly revise their outdated methods of observing and understanding natural design, which are limited by learning from only superficial appearances in our theatrical consciousness. While mainly depending on the appearances augmented through super microscopes or super telescopes, built after our physical eyes, our visions are unavoidably "landing" on stages of our superficial consciousness.

Why is it that our technology does not manifest the true presence of human intelligence but, on the contrary, reveals how poor human abilities are constantly challenged within fluctuating environmental conditions? Technologies today serve more or less as crutches for human beings who cannot fly, run, or swim fast enough, and who cannot develop protective fur, shells, or feathers, great vision, hearing, not even great teeth. Humans poorly see, hear or smell when compared to the majority of animals. Our use of our technologies shows how extremely needy and eventually helpless we become as human beings, both physically and mentally.

What critical understanding is still missing from our knowledge of our existence? To recognize the most powerful and absolutely unavoidable conditions of the world, which are present in our mundane life—in our visions or dreams, memories, and thinking–whether we categorize our experience as common, artistic, scientific, philosophical, physical, or mental—we do not need any technology.

It is very important to admit that everything we may observe in the superficial stages of what we recognize as human "consciousness" is already instinctively *processed through our very limited sensory perceptions.*

Imagine that our consciousness is actually highly superficial, similar to the flat screens of computers and TVs, such that our perceptions catch our primary "sparks" of sensations as signals on the surface of a somewhat flattish consciousness. The sensations create sparks of energies in our mind consciousness. They work like the signals or "pixels" that are composed on a computer screen. The mind processes instances of sensations into compositions of appearances that are observable to us within.

As we focus on human physical or bodily organs they are resembling us some organic "devices." These remain greatly under-developed, and unlike animals and other living beings in the wild, when we greatly depend on these organs, we are very poorly coordinated in life, in the wilderness, and even in our artificial "isolation" from numerous natural conditions that we build within our communities, villages, towns, and cities as long as for millennia, and commuting via artificial road systems with road signs for easy communication suitable for human needs. Except for human beings, no form of life needs maps, compasses, clocks, clothing, manufactured food, Wi-Fi, automobiles, jets, rockets, or any other technology for communication, nor do they need artificially produced energy, artificial entertainment, "weather reports," or the "news." Even when we try very hard to compensate for our great human limitations and obstacles in life by building artificial devices augmenting our corporeal sight or hearing, as well as building complicated but rather clumsy vessels for sea, air, and space travel, when compared to nature's original living design, these super-gadgets remain primitive and unsafe, and the same problems remain as our bodies are not naturally equipped with faculties for flying or swimming etc., on their own. Manipulating our bodies to the extreme as we do is abysmally unwise when we compare this with an appreciation for the innate skill and aptitude of nature's creations.

With our great pride in all our technological achievements, we only become more opinionated rather than truly knowledgeable—and in many cases, while depending on tech gadgets, our minds become lazier; we are subject to nature's ever-changing conditions and challenges, but we hardly notice them until disasters "suddenly" Strike. For instance, while using wireless gadgets, we can now reach each other across great distances but still cannot understand each other any better than we could millennia ago. We continue to argue, fight, and mindlessly destroy things as living beings trying to manipulate nature's design and struggle to replace it lacking a true understanding of what we are dealing with.

Our artificial human language, based on conventionally assembled systems of symbols, images, and sounds that form words and images of words, requires training to be perceived, understood, and used as a supposedly meaningful form of communication. This remains the prevailing method of sharing our seemingly collective ideas. However, nothing can be perceived or understood directly and perfectly in the same way that others perceive and understand it; our perceptions are unique. Do we need to relearn to communicate among ourselves? When we exchange our experiences through artificially invented and established languages consisting of uniform groups of signs, symbols, sounds, and images, our personal living experiences are easily misunderstood, and the original meaning is twisted in different ways within different minds. We are not born speaking our man-made languages but have to learn them by mimicking adults. Perhaps mimicking abilities prevail over all the other abilities that many of us may possess.

Before expressing ourselves in human language, we must hear, see, and process symbolic words in our personal imagination while preliminarily reviewing the meanings of these language symbols in our minds. We also try to predict some actions, our own and those of others, by playing scenarios in our imagination before we speak and act. Thus, it takes seconds, or much longer, to articulate our thoughts or feelings, especially when we compare our own language-based communications to immediate instinctive communications among other forms of life, spontaneously exchanging intuitive sensations they are personally experiencing within natural environments and commonly in any distances.

Under the most powerful law of *Flux*, nothing can be truly and absolutely left unchanged, reflected, copied, repeated, or duplicated as it was before. We change entirely while we interact and communicate.

There is no equality or equity for all, but endless possibilities of creative harmonious coexistence for the sake of vitality. This is the fundamental condition of God's creative nature.

CHAPTER 5

No man-made law is truly powerful enough to withstand nature's power.

The world of *Flux* is an endlessly harmonious orchestra against cacophonies storming its nature, where we learn to sense and recognize harmonies, and make our choices. Whether we are gifted with good ears and sing along as wondrous single instruments or carelessly produce loud cacophonies destroying ourselves screaming in desperation until we lose our own singing voices, we are all granted some blessed creative abilities that are hidden deeply inside us. These blessed abilities are tuned to the vitality of nature, leading us to safety and meaningful survival.

We are naturally born with deep primary intuition, similar to all other living beings. Intuition, like an internal compass in our intimately ever-new and ever-changing environment, leads us to act in accordance with change in our circumstances.

As we grow up, we begin to suppress this inborn intuition. Starting from our early childhood training, education, and practice in mimicking adults, we become little players in the societal playhouse, struggling to fit and serve stiff man-made mode of life, habits and fake beliefs. It is debatable whether our human society is still tribal or more complex, or whether we have developed our wisdom based on our beliefs or have borrowed teachings from other older cultures and only manipulated it, mindlessly abusing the original meaning, into just instructions that are sometimes extreme and cultish; nonetheless, as soon as we are trained enough to adapt to these artificial constructs that unify and control our beliefs, minds, bodies, and lifestyles, we find ourselves locked up inside confusing and even destructive human activities. We commonly mistake what we observe and see for the objective world, and then our world becomes too small as we are struggling to fit poor man-made culture, systems, models, and judgments.

In the first place, however, our sensory perceptions are not designed to directly see, touch, or hear anything as it is "out there." If we were directly exposed to everything, as mentioned above, we would melt away in no time in a world of ever-changing instants. We need our specific limitations, which are conditions that I suggest we should view not just as obstacles, but as *protective boundaries* for life.

We are here to discover comprehensive explanations for the fascinating nature of our world and keep discovering the as-yet ungrasped Flux itself, the most vital source of our existence. Even with our limited ability to perceive our realities, we can still deeply sense some new irreversible conditions within and without. However, no one can reflect on anything just as it is, as nothing remains as it was exactly an instant ago.

Yet, how do we actually recognize ourselves, "separating" ourselves from the rest of the spectacles, backgrounds, and objects that are visible to us? Why is it that we ourselves are never objective observers?

These questions can be answered in our new field of knowledge of the nature of the mind, showing its endless wonders and possibilities as we begin to comprehend and explore ourselves in unexampled or unparalleled ways.

To understand, learn about, and evolve our minds, we need to begin by carefully revising our existing basic education, which lacks the very foundation of human knowledge we are yet to build. To establish new cross-sector interactive schools for sharing experiences, learning, and practicing our innovative approach toward advanced education, no capital such as accumulated wealth or money is needed. Classical gatherings for sharing knowledge and experience, such as in ancient schools where teachers and students of all sorts gather to exchange what they know and think, can be organized anywhere.

"The sun is new each day," as the great sage Heraclitus asserted, explaining the concept of Flux as early as c. 535–475 BC. Heraclitus is the most profound thinker in our short history; his teachings continue to enlighten us with fundamental knowledge of the nature of the world and the most powerful laws we may experience in it. However, he has not been understood for millennia. It is very inconvenient for us, as humans, to accept the obvious fact that change is instantly "transforming" us, our minds, and bodies, into new minds and bodies before we can blink. Though Flux is an unavoidable condition everywhere, and we watch our stubborn struggle to build permanent, fixed, and balanced systems or manufacture "perfect things"—dreaming about unbreakable societies under man-made rules, all that is destined to be doomed even before we begin to build them. Small diverse systems are easy to fix and improve when they are interactive; if they collapse, we replace them locally with better varieties without causing great destruction to the earth, as colossal artificially built systems unavoidably do.

We are all on an endless journey of playful living selves.

Before we can even sense something, the magnificent world of Flux entirely transforms it into an entirely new ephemeral composition. We have no time to notice the metamorphic existence of the world we inhabit.

Our uniquely limited perceptions of our realities allow us to interpret our circumstances and become responsible for our own existence. Our interacting "tools" are our *perceptions* manifesting the existence of our life—that is the most creative *process* we may ever experience and know.

The unthinkable Flux keeps affecting our minds and bodies beyond our comprehension, as the world is perpetually changing its conditions within less than an instant; it cannot "wait" and "freeze" itself to allow us to see, photograph, or record and store any segment of it in any permanent format, not even in our fantasies, which must instantly change to continue our dreams and thoughts. We observe only our own limitedly rendered impressions of realities we may experience.

I believe that our basic artistic abilities are granted to us by nature for a much greater purpose than to create art as we know it. Our sensations are living colorful paints, our feelings are brushes, and our intuition empowers the artist's creative Self. The mind is an artist, always in the process of interpreting what it senses as events, characters, landscapes, and even animated stories. No photography or video technology can replace the artistic abilities internally granted to us to create ourselves freely from the core of our characters. The intuitive and fertile creativity of a living mind is the source of life. No any other sort of energy a mind is ever needed but its very own production.

The mind creates energies from perceiving immense instances of change, but still awards itself by only hopelessly poor visions. However, we can randomly create amusing imagination and magnificent spectacles in mind. This is how *Nature's living mechanism of perceptions* propels our unique realities.

CHAPTER 6

This primordial mental *mechanism of perceptions* has been unnoticed for millennia, but it amusingly demonstrates its routine in the process of painting a classical work of art. While painting, a classical artist constantly *compares, selects, and focuses* on something that seems important, overlaying it on a vague background of the mind. The artist then *frames* his finished work, separating it from all disturbances created by the surroundings of all sorts; our minds operate similarly. This explains why we perceive our realities similarly. However, our bodies are only temporary mind experience. A mind is an artist, actor, student and teacher, all in one. The mind catches its random sensations in its net-fabric like consciousness.

Painting on flat surfaces is guided by the deep intuitive behavior of the mind. The theatrical consciousness that we develop on the stages of our imagination is separated from the depths of our minds. Every mind goes through the classical artist's routine, and this instinctive mental routine is endlessly present in us, whether we are observing, thinking about, memorizing, or imagining something, or whether we are awake or asleep.

We are taking a step into the unknown field of the mind's nature, heading toward a new era of breakthrough discoveries that can neither fit inside labs nor actual brains, cannot be explained by fixed equations, and cannot be detected through any man-made device.

We are about to discover our mind's natural abilities responsible for creating its visualization in "consciousness," where our pictorial imagination thrives, while building its fantastic scenarios of what we sense and understand as our realities. While we are noticing how our primary *nature's mechanism of perceptions allows us to Compare, Select, Compose, Focus, and even "frame" our mental productions from just instances of our sensations we discover the very living mind*. The Natural Mechanism of Perceptions is endlessly empowered by the unavoidable laws of Flux.

Perception is a principal drive creating all our sensations, feelings, visions and motivation in thinking, learning and acting. The very process of perception eventually empowers life.

Nature's mechanism of perceptions is what all forms of life have in common, that is, in our mutual instinctive effort to thrive and survive within the conditions of the unstoppable Flux.

Every life change, minuscule or grand, is limited in many ways, and all our limitations play a crucial role in revealing nature's wonders of its protective boundaries saving our existence from complete dissolution into the overwhelming powers of Flux, whether we are aware of these protective boundaries, or take these as obstacles or even a curse. Only a few notes remain from the great philosopher of antiquity, Protagoras, on his contemplations of *limitations* as an inseparable crucial function of the entire condition of Flux. His writings were banned and eventually destroyed by the authorities of his time.

To further develop the fundamental and immortal thoughts of thinkers such as Heraclitus and Protagoras on the unavoidable laws of universal nature, I suggest beginning with contemplation of *nature's living mechanism of perceptions, within our own mind*, which reveals to us why our entire existence, though uniquely personal, is inseparable from and depends entirely on the instant and irreversible worlds of playhouses of creative nature. This is how we travel these worlds.

Our human history is still at the dawn of its existence.

I invite every curious reader—and I still hope to find one or two—to join this pioneering study beyond the closed "spaces" of existing histories, institutions, laboratories, and technologies, beyond exciting appearances through super microscopes or telescopes where the long-outdated, entangled, and confused human knowledge has been recycling while misleading our psyche, mentalities, ideas, and deeds for millennia.

CHAPTER 7

In this chapter, I would like to share a discovery that struck me in a most unprecedented way. At that time, I was still a teen artist and not able to find any knowledge of this "artistic" behavior of my mind anywhere. It took me some time to find out that this kind of knowledge did not exist.

While painting a still life in my art class in an old academic art school, I noticed that while depicting my work on canvas, I kept comparing, selecting, focusing on, and composing images in my mind repeatedly while painting them on my canvas.

I noticed that I kept following this as a sort of routine, first in my mind, instinctively, as all artists do; however, I received no school instruction of this kind.

I then had to admit that my mind unstoppably explored this artist's routine beyond my comprehension, while *observing*, *memorizing*, *learning*, *thinking*, *calculating*, and *dreaming*, whether I was awake or asleep.

I first wondered whether I was subnormal, but after thinking about this idea day and night and watching other people, I had to conclude that none of us could stop comparing, selecting, focusing, and composing our impressions of our environments into ever-changing visions, just like a painter. All that we do begins with mental activities of various sorts. Even when suffering a sudden bodily injury, the mind cannot immediately sense pain. Rather, the mind takes time to instinctively process the initial sensations of its interaction with the body affected by the pain. Pain, joy, and all the other primary sensations related to bodies must first be perceived in the mind.

Something then grabbed my attention in that art class. Why is this very easily noticeable artist's routine, which has been used instinctively or intuitively for millennia in prehistoric and traditional art, never been recognized as a major function of the mind? This unstoppable mental artist's routine activates our senses. Without it, we cannot perceive, communicate, memorize, think, or dream. Each living mind behaves as a subconscious or primordial artist in every one of us, activating the very process of its existence and making it intimately and uniquely personal within oneself.

I decided to share my overwhelming thoughts with my art teacher. I was painfully shy when tried to clumsily explain that art is not a human invention. Our minds must possess inborn, instinctive abilities to observe reality in a manner similar to the routines that all artists follow while painting. Our minds clearly demonstrate what kind of mental processes literally *makes* us see, think, memorize, imagine, and dream. Just like any classically trained painter, our deeply instinctive minds keep *comparing*, *selecting*, *focusing*, and *composing* randomly selected subjects and images of what we believe we look at "out there." In our minds, we "frame" subjects of our observation in groups, just as we frame thoughts by isolating them from the rest of what we keep in our minds. In this way, we strive to create some sort of order in our minds to make things observable in a coherent composition. As we need to compare what we sense, we easily discover that we cannot see just one thing separately on its own, unrelated to anything else. Comparison: this is how our minds unstoppably create their internal environment by connecting not only sensations but also visions as groups of multiple images, as well as combinations of thoughts and ideas, including seemly restrictive mathematics and the sciences, philosophy, and literature. The artist's routine is unavoidable. As it is impossible for us to truly see anything separately on its own, we must instinctively "shoot" and continuously change our focus on what attracts or disturbs us, putting the rest to linger in a deep vague background. One can recognize how memories emerge from these lingering backgrounds of our living thoughts.

Why do we perceive in spite of we still never see anything as it is "out there?" The clearest thoughts in philosophy over the past several hundred years have been led by the intuitively brilliant logic of George Berkeley on the idea of a "thing in itself," discussed in his 1713 work *Three Dialogues Between Hylas and Philonous*. (Immanuel Kant only borrowed Berkeley's original idea of a "thing in itself").

After his pioneering philosophical writing, *Three Dialogues Between Hylas and Philonous*, Berkeley simply stopped thinking about any further explanation. He only refers everything to the Creator's *will*. I think, however, despite Berkeley's idea that the Creator puts everything in our minds, exploring all the grand creative powers *He* possesses, it is impossible that the Creator would bother to put countless mundane, silly, pretty, ugly, bloody, confusing, or simply stupid visions and ideas in our minds. Therefore, I posit that it is easier to understand why we are so generously granted the wondrous tools of perception, that allow us to be free to learn to create on our own as little creators. We can discover and learn from our natural basic abilities to create our visions looking for our ways in our ever-changing existence. The mind is a little creator for the sake of its vitality and evolution.

CHAPTER 8

We cannot observe anything directly and instantly, and we cannot set things or living beings in our minds just as they are out there. "Things in themselves" neither fit our minds, nor brains. Even the physical sensations that we think we effortlessly feel must somehow be assimilated. We are able to observe only what we are able to mentally process by digesting random sensations through perception. Our visions are unique impressions composed of our experiences, together with ever-changing sensations emerging like the instant sparks of living energies. Sparks of our energies: what we feel as "material" or "physical" is the result of our mental work, affected by temporary crude and random interactions with what we observe as a "physical" body, which is an organic composition of myriads of different life forms. These forms of life contain living minds on their own.

Whether rich or poor, our minds are "cooking" not only what we perceive and sense as our reality but also producing the impressions we express in symbolic forms, similar to expressions of the primordial artist who at first has processed his creative imagination in his mind before depicting it on the flattish surfaces of his cave walls. Symbolic, simplified or deducted images form shows us the first stage of human language development.

When affected by the conditions of the body, the mind creates its internal, temporary, theatrical, and superficial "consciousness" of spectacles, where the body is acting as a visible entity to the mind, as long as it can sense a body.

This means that only the mind is the creator of visions of its "reality universes," and no brain or any other bodily organ is able to compose and observe any of our visions. Our minds are responsible for processing all our ever-fluctuating sensations. Whether while receiving bodily signals or on their own, our minds follow their subconscious routine behavior of *comparing, selecting, focusing, composing, and framing* initial abstract impressions and sensations, and as an artist turning them into visions. Just like any art pieces these can be poor, silly, funny, horrific, or harmoniously beautiful. No surgeon, researcher, or butcher has ever seen any image, thought, word, or number in a brain. The brain is only a bodily sensory organ and cannot perceive on its own. You can enjoy, or be healed, or destroyed by what your mind can stage for you.

Unlike an artist, the mind cannot stop *comparing, selecting, focusing, and composing*, whether we are awake, asleep, dreaming, thinking, or memorizing. This process is inseparable from the existence of ourselves as selves. ***It reveals that the blessed act of perceiving is the most basic process of life.*** By willingly changing our mind's perceptions based on our experiences, we may be able to greatly enrich, revive, and reinvent our very existence.

A few days after thinking over this young artist's unprecedented observation, I told my art teacher: "I think that the mind is a primordial artist living within ourselves."

As we fail to recognize our internal abilities of perception, we fail to grasp the very process of our observing and thinking.

We try to express ourselves through human language, behavior, and what we call ideas, rendered in the arts, sciences, or philosophy, with no clue about what makes our realities possible for us. The *living mechanism of perceptions* remains hidden behind the curtains of our temporary mental theater of superficial human consciousness, where we prefer to stage, observe and judge the appearances of what we believe reality is.

These realities are unique products of our minds' perceptions and interpretations of our life experiences of ourselves. One mind is one interpreter of life for each person.

Whether we believe that we may see the actual world with aliens, monsters and angels, or robotic systems independently floating in the universe, our sensations are strictly personal, unique instances of our primary and abstract interactions, without and within our minds. We cannot ever repeat instances of our lives, but in different ways, we do create our expressions of what we uniquely feel and experience. Judging the world based on our impressions processed in our temporary theatrical consciousness would keep us in the dark ages of recurring human history.

The world is difficult to understand in terms of *Flux* for adults; however, this great ancient philosophical notion is still inborn and roving in each of our minds since infancy, when we still were newcomers from another "dimension" and did not have to become great philosophers to sense the majestic transformations of everything inside and around us.

Heraclitus's timeless discovery, which he articulates in his poetic depictions of the colossal *Flux*, is an unavoidable condition of all conditions.

For the first time, I suggest trying to comprehend the deeply intuitive *mechanism of perception of our minds interacting* with the metamorphosis of *Flux*.

CHAPTER 9

We commonly recognize our mind as the soul or spirit, whose natural functions now explain, based on a process of perception, how endlessly creative our possibilities may become.

The mechanism of perceptions is not mechanical, but its functions can nonetheless be explained clearly, as we may feel them instinctively in every moment. Based on this most essential mental process of assimilating our primary, immediate, and instantly immerging sensations from which every mind builds its wonders of existence, each living entity recognizes its reality after some experience has already been uniquely staged within its mind. Every form of life that we commonly observe, even just as the appearance of some physical body, possesses a unique mind, which creates its intimate personal and unique reality.

What can be a more precious gift from God for a believer than the blessed freedom to exist and evolve as your Self while learning to create and exploring your inborn abilities of a little creator? Granted the freedom to create and recreate oneself one is learning about the world after the wisdom of one's spiritual parent. If you fail, try again under any condition. Each life is originally thriving in a living process of self-development or evolution, and these possibilities are open not only to every one of us human beings but also to all life forms.

As living beings, we can build unique sovereign realities and characters that no one but ourselves can truly destroy.

Back in my art class, I remember how, after I spoke with my kind art teacher trying to think over my new clumsy but striking teenage observations. I was unable to accurately articulate my overwhelming experience. My art teacher knew that I had been studying classical philosophy since I was 11 years old and he loved discussing classical and contemporary ideas in art and life with me. However, that new conversation about the nature of our perceptions working together as an ephemeral mechanism within our minds felt very special for both of us. A few days later, my art teacher told me that he believed I was not only a promising art student but also a little philosopher and that I should write down my ideas, at least as notes, no matter how clumsy these notes might be. I followed his thoughtful advice and have never regretted it. From that very day, I started writing down on random pieces of paper and even napkins—my abbreviated thoughts, which I later developed in the work *An Artist's Notes.*

Something that is new and unknown is extremely difficult to formulate in common language or a traditional professional format. It is much easier to criticize new thoughts by gluing them to categories of already known topics discovered by previously established authors. I presume that my work will never be accepted as is. However, I have noticed that the truly pioneering works in history were never beautifully or perfectly expressed and performed. In the fields of mathematics, physics, research, literature, and philosophy, as well as in classical art, innovative works did not look as greatly polished, organized, and refined as the works of their followers, who did not need to discover or invent anything new again but could instead work on polishing new skills in their presentation of others' remarkable ideas, as revealed by the original pioneers.

How do we learn while exploring our perception of *comparison*, and why is it critical? While our young, still very clumsy, bodies are developing, and before we take our first steps on the ground and pronounce our first words, we intuitively begin to explore our inborn talents of a primordial creative artist. This artist is already residing within our ephemeral young minds.

A very young child swims in an endless ocean of instant-by-instant sensations. Not just Heraclitus but every living being has this primordial experience from birth. As one's mind feels its first impressions through new interactions with a tiny newly developing body, one keeps comparing one's first vague abstract sensations while still becoming familiar with one's somewhat alien, young, and undeveloped body.

The instinct of *comparison* is a primary function of every living being, and that is why a human *mind* slowly learns. Every mind learns to feel its new child's body that needs years to grow up "physically," still experiencing how to explore bodily functional sensory organs to see, hear, and collate one's first corporeal impressions, through this yet "unexperienced" young body with one head, one mouth, one nose, two ears, two eyes, two legs, and two arms, etc. Nature has granted us these living tools for exploring our existences in manifold ways.

It takes time for the mind of an infant to be able to sense the new world through its physical organs, such as the eyes, while differentiating its still-blurry impressions of the mother's hand, comparing it with her lips and her voice pronouncing unfamiliar words filled with love. The first non-physical mentally perceived sensations that penetrate the young body are striking.

Mental *comparison* is our most vital, basic ability in life; while perceiving a very young body, it animates our so-called entirely new (to the young individual) physical movements based on our sensations and feelings. This physical experience may be shocking at first, occurring at a stage when we cannot yet talk. Thus, babies cry.

Why is it that the mental process of comparing our forever variable impressions is *unstoppable,* whether we are awake or asleep, memorizing, or thinking? If we cannot compare our mental sensations, we will feel no differences in our experiences and in our bodies, as they then become senseless and fail to exist—the death of the brain and the rest of the body follows when a mind stops *comparing bodily sensations.*

Our bodily functions become paralyzed when they are disconnected from the mind. Interactions between the mind and body mutually ignite their energies so that they act as living magnets, attracting one another. In rare cases, the deep physical stress created by our overwhelming, physical sensations storming through the body can eventually paralyze all our corporeal sensory organs and, similar to an electric shock, cause complete bodily dysfunction and physical death.

While alive, our bodies are interconnected throughout affected by our mental functions, keeping our temporary bodies alive as one organism.

Constantly energized and affected by sensations, our memories are like Heraclitus' River, always running as they are transforming. Though memory has some continuity, we cannot experience the same sensations, feelings, and therefore, memories twice. Memories seemingly flow in their ephemeral moment-by-moment transformations. Memories are never fixed but are ever-changing in their flow, thus constantly transforming the rest of our Selves, just like Heraclitus' River.

Our mentally produced sensations create powerful fields that keep our realities together.

As these internal fields of primary sensations affect what we may observe and feel, they are similar to what we describe as magnetic fields in physics. No physical reality can exist on its own. Specific sensations that we experience while interacting with the world around us using our body, which we feel and call physical conditions, are not "objective conditions."

We must possess living minds to experience sensations in ever-changing formations, including the visions of magnetic fields within our minds—the perceivers. We cannot discover magnetic fields or their nature if we have no sensations. Under the power of Flux, there is no time to keep anything together in any instant composition. Flux is instantaneous metamorphosis. Our minds have the gift of composing themselves from the powers of constant change, producing unique fields of internal wonder realities.

When we begin searching for the basic functions of the mind (not the brain), we can be astonished at how the possibilities and abilities of the mind, naturally granted to every living being from birth, enable us to survive by transforming and recreating ourselves. Unlike humans, many living beings (e.g., jellyfish, corals, trees, plants, or mushrooms) do not require a brain to sense their ever-transforming environment. These transformations are deeply metamorphic as all expediencies of physical reality, its physical laws, and the "material" feelings of them, all that begins from our ephemeral fluctuating instances of mental sensations.

The greatest confusion we human beings face in dealing with life is not outside ourselves, but within.

No mind can leave itself to observe anything in the mighty world beyond itself. If one were to escape from one's self into an outer existence of the colossal powers of Flux, one would melt away like a tiny lump of sugar in a cup of very hot tea. No spaceship can ever take us outside ourselves to see the universe objectively, because a spaceship only carries bodies, moreover, we sense bodies traveling into the cosmic landscapes perceived and therefore, become visible only inside minds.

Findings in physics, chemistry, and even psychology tell us that scholars and theorists in these fields are missing the presence of themselves in all they have been observing, analyzing, and describing, commonly imagining possible objectivity in their contemplations and modeling.

First, each of our minds is a unique perceiver and *observer. Nature's mechanism of perceptions* of the mind eventually shows that it is not the brain that produces thoughts as a physical liver produces bile, as a popular materialistic idea proposes.

CHAPTER 10

Every mind naturally possesses its primordial art, sound recording, and animation studios, all in its creative "chamber," and none of our so-called inventions/creations, such as the visual arts, theatrical performances, movies, recordings, technologies of any kind, are truly our human invention.

No technology or science can answer where our minds are and how our minds observe and think, creating visions of what we sense and feel as reality. As a mere bodily transmitter, the brain cannot produce an actual image or thought. **Minds are not observable by other spectators.** They are observers within themselves as unique sovereign entities.

Although based on using similar physical sensory or bodily perceptions that we might sense in our *collectively described* experiences, we never truly sense anything in exactly the same way, as our minds are entirely unique to live as individual selves, not just one mind. Each of our realities has its own internal universe composed of our productions of it. Human experience cannot be objective; when combined, our information remains only approximately *collective* and *not objective.*

In protecting our own existence, as well as everything else that may exist, we experience great *limitations*. A contemporary of Heraclitus, the philosopher Protagoras, revealed and contemplated the endless limitations of everything that might exist. We shall learn that *limitations* are just as changeable, as they are always attuned to the powers of *Flux*. Despite the world conditions of opposites (which have been described by Heraclitus), opposites are never equal, possessing a tendency toward *unbalancing* conditions of all sorts. Flux never allows any perfect balance that we dream about in our unreal models of structured systems, such as math and engineering.

Only an unbalanced reality is ever possible for living beings to exist in, and any existences, including ours as human beings, are entirely involved, interwoven, and dependent on mutually creating new environments out of more or less unbalanced opposites.

The nature of such unavoidable change makes us face ever new and different *limitations*. Protagoras' writing was destroyed by the ignorant rulers of his time along with his life, leaving only a few original notes. These notes have been mentioned in Plato's critical writing toward concepts of Flux and limitations ever transforming the world, as these powerful notions destroy his famous *fixed forever ideals*. However, Heraclitus' Flux and Protagoras' Limitations intrigued thinking minds to this day.

In accordance with Protagoras' outstanding and vital ideas, we may extrapolate his thoughts and observe that even a very young child feels, just like adults ourselves, that everything sensed is somehow more or less *limited*, like everything we interact with. This reveals *resistance* of all types, that we sense physically and mentally. Even when some resistance remains invisible, we feel that we "touch" something, or what we may feel as some "tangible objects" somehow more or less resist us. **However, the sensation of resistance implies *limitations.***

Limitations frame our ephemeral, uniquely singular experience, which means that the productions of the mind are shaped by limitations within our personal characteristics.

Only through *limitations* are we able to produce sensations, feelings, memories, and thoughts and pursue related activities and deeds of all kinds. **The entire lack of limitations means we become nothing.**

Our sensations that we feel as resistance and our experiences of them identify emerging varieties of obstacles of all sorts. Whether painful, joyful, or anything in between, we cannot sense anything without mutual resistance toward what we are already interacting with.

We reside in the existence of opposites and resistance of different natures. Going through potentially endless transformations of Flux, everything is limited simply in order to exist as itself, while being more or less unbalanced to allow new changes to continue.

I would suggest that we observe our limitations not merely as hindrances but as nature's gifts, obstacles that we do not need to always fight but can comprehend and creatively apply to our current reality by changing our behavior and old habits and finding beneficial conditions, mainly internally within our bodies and minds, as the most intuitive living beings do in nature. Nature's *limitations* or resistances, which we endlessly face, mainly serve as our *protective boundaries* that guard us against possible destruction that we are unaware of.

Nature's limitations are like a sculptor's chisel carving us—as living characters of human beings, as well as everything else that exists —out of the infinite metamorphoses of the world.

By continuing to evolve within our myriad limitations stimulating our creativity our work becomes endless and vividly inspirational in its nature, the essence of the nature's art of life.

Within our ever-differing circumstances, we are never the same, proving how tremendous the creativity of life is. Life is forever surprising us with new turns, even though it might seem to us the same. Our descriptions of the variety of sensations, such as resistance or limitations, have the following effect on us: activating attraction or magnetic-like compositions of our sensations into experiences from playful opposites, as pointed out by Heraclitus. These sensations would not be able to create our realities without our minds, and their life-producing inborn ability to constantly *compare, select, focus, compose, and recompose* these sensations. Whether poor or immensely rich, life is continuous creativity.

As we use certain devices to augment our extremely underdeveloped bodily organs, we collect increasingly detailed visions of our previous visions and, ironically, reprocess them through the same initially undeveloped corporeal sensory organs. Technologies are limited to serving our physical sensory organs. These technologies only act as our artificial crutches to "explore the world," which do not take us any farther from our human body and still millennia-old basic bodily or physical experience.

Endless forms of life do not perceive what we observe as our visible reality, and obviously do not see us, humans, as something important. For instance, we can see, touch, and measure a wooden desk, but some different forms of life, such as bacteria or viruses, do not even perceive it as a desk, not to mention our own human presence. These tiny beings face no obstacles in passing right through the desk, ignoring its shape, color, texture, and smell, as these characteristics do not exist in their reality. The desk is not "material" either for tiny bacteria or for the world. The desk's "solid" composition is what we sense through our perception that literally creates physical feelings and related visions of what we sense as the desk.

CHAPTER 11

The laws of physics that we learn in schools and deal within our mundane lives are not universal in a world of endlessly unique existences. These laws we study in physics do not exist in the metamorphic Flux. The colossal powers of universal nature are overlooked in our education entirely because these laws initially are not recognized as "physical." We pay attention to what we uniquely sense through our human bodies. However, I would be grateful if my childhood teachers had been able to explain to me that the physical laws we describe and apply in our lives only manifest very limited and specific human conditions of what we call physical or bodily experience. In the worlds of Flux, myriad living organisms have no need for anything such as observations of the planet Earth, Sun, and stars within the "system" of the universe. Different living beings sense the world in myriad interpretations that we would never know.

Bodies are combinations of ephemeral forms of life-producing energy that comprise fields of interactive sensations in the mind. Perhaps what we understand as magnetic fields, as articulated by the great Michael Faraday, are not independent forces external to our minds. Perhaps what we perceive as the cosmos is the result of our minds creating spectacles and impressions processed from our sensations that obviously would not be possible to observe outside our minds—the masters of our realities. Perhaps these energies creating magnetic- like fields outside our minds and bodies from which we may interact, sense, and produce within our internal process of perception are *the opposites*—changes rejecting, attracting, and uniting powers.

It seems that Heraclitus's description of instances of *Flux*, always ignited by the energies of *the opposites*, might point to what we sense and experience as electric fields. The functions of electric currents in contemporary technology–producing electric energy that affects our everyday lives–are what we all experience as they are processed through our fascinating powers of mental perceptions.

Surviving and evolving uniquely within the colossal powers of the world, the human mind struggles to find the self in the world unobservable to it. While striving to prolong our existence every moment, we must step into new rivers of worlds that are different to us—not just one world, but many.

The human consciousness of "tangible" appearances cannot reflect these myriad worlds. One's reality where one may feel most comfortable as the self is one's authentic sovereign home.

CHAPTER 12

How can we express and share our visions of our own mind? The first artist, a "caveman," demonstrated this by discovering that he could depict some lines and contouring images of visibly familiar shapes on the flattish area on the walls of his cave. A caveman primitively outlined images from his memories that defined the edges of their form. These lines were among the first drawings in human history, a type of art familiar to us as two-dimensional depictions of three-dimensional objects or scenes.

The lines drawn by such early artists somehow became recognizable to our perceptions today, as we have the same "mechanism" of perception as we had millions of years ago. The cave art and the lines depicted on the cave walls were perceived by the rest of the cave artist's tribe or family as something familiar, resembling similar experiences rendered in memories. This tells us that some sketchy images of symbolic lines on a wall have provoked other human minds, while using similar human physical sensory organs, to recognize some shapes by even projecting these simple line drawings and animating them as living characters in each of their own minds. By projecting crude lines onto the imagination and into active stories related to the onlooker's experience, we may share the most fascinating exchange of visions and thoughts. This primordial art reveals a mental process in our instinctive mind, very similar to how we use manmade visible symbols in languages and, beginning later, groups of signs in mathematics and the compositions of symbols in the sciences. The human mental process of perception is always at the inner root of communication and learning.

We still prefer flat surfaces for depicting impressions using paper, canvas, photos, screens, maps, and other surfaces for writing, reading, and illustrating. Our habit of collecting impressions on surfaces leads us to conclusions about the existence of curious spaces, distances, and perspectives that are absolutely impossible within the nature of Flux, as timeless and spaceless instants of Flux have no true time, distances, and therefore no space. We build these temporary conditions in our imagination of sensations from which we compose the playhouses of consciousness.

To prolong our imaginable ephemeral impressions, at least for a while, we instinctively or intentionally find ways to construct and reconstruct similar images in multiple positions, building "perspective" views for these images. However, we can do so only in superficial theatrical and ephemeral consciousness. Perspective, as we further understand, means the imaginative composition of images in the dimensional "stability" of space, which is impossible according to the forever unstable nature of Flux. *Nature's mechanism of perceptions* of the mind plays not only a crucially important role in our entire existence but is also the primary artistic source of our amusing fantasies or productions of what we eventually build to share with others. We call some forms of these expressions "entertainment."

While composing visions, our minds are "framing" them into groups of images, similar to framed art pieces. In order to animate the images in them we run them similarly to how we are *animating these images* in a movie. Henri Bergson intuitively discovered the similarity between the effect of the duration we see in movies and our perceiving minds creating visible continuity of constantly fluctuating images. This major development of Henri Bergson in understanding human perceptions of movement has not been truly understood; rather, he received the Nobel Prize for Literature in 1927 for his work *Creative Evolution*.

The wonder of perceiving is a deeply instinctive process of life happening behind the thick mental curtains of the theater of our consciousness. However, it is not difficult to watch how our minds instinctively process fleeting mental impressions into effects of duration, which creates depths of distance by changing related impressions that we try to connect and run through this movie-like rolling-frames mental process.

Later, we will explore how we "calculate" the speed of light as an "objective" phenomenon while entirely missing the mental process of our own perceiving. **The speed of light we perceive is revealing our own limited human speed of perceptions.** The speed of light we may measure reveals only the speed of our own corporeal sight. The human perception of physical sight is the most elusive, slippery, and misleading corporeal sensory perception we possess. Merleau-Ponty has been one of the Western philosophers most intrigued by the body as a medium of the primary physical site and the source for our "knowing the world." Since the time of Descartes and Locke, who struggled to comprehend the nature of what we believe consciousness may be and whether it is the only way for us to exist in the world, we, right now, may use different methods to approach the most profound experience of knowing, however, when we respect and learn from the fundamental conditions of Flux.

Remarkably, in his fundamental work *Phenomenology of Perception*, Maurice *Merleau-Ponty* mercilessly exposed and proved the instability and deceptiveness of what we actually *see* based on our perceptions through physical organs.

All questions on perception remain most intriguing in what is called continental as well as in analytical philosophy, still missing the presence of our own minds in all our possible observations. Moreover, this gap in knowledge concerning the fact that our perceptions are never fixed and cannot truly express reality as something exact or perfect leaves professional researchers confused.

From Heisenberg's revelation of the observer effect, we learn the impossibility of observing anything "objectively." Moreover, no one is able to observe anything without affecting and disturbing the objects of one's observations. However, in common thought and specifically in physics and the rest of the sciences, this grand basic knowledge toward our observations has been twisted for the convenience of the previously established idea blindly relying on nonexistent "objectivity."

From the researchers in labs and in the fields of experiments to the average public who easily adopts popular sketchy opinions, the majority are still unable to admit the absolute impossibility of our "objectivity." The ignorance of this sort commonly provokes researchers, scholars, or authorities at all levels and in all fields to be very sure of their own "calculated objectiveness." Moreover, this false confidence is directly related to our human tragedy rooted in our continuous ignorance in general knowledge blindly leading us to myriad small and eventually catastrophic mistakes.

The *observer* effect explains the disturbance of an observed system by the act of *observation*. This crucial knowledge is beyond our basic understanding of our limitations and the functions of our personal and unique sensory perceptions, without which no knowledge can exist at all. Perceptions are possible and functional only with the unavoidable act of momentary interactions.

The lack of awareness among ignorant people who are teaching, governing, and even enforcing mindlessly blind conclusions also makes them unaware of their violating others. Moreover, when interfering in the lives of other unique living beings, these "authorities" in all fields ignore the factual presence of themselves while often acting as uninvited mind-blind intruders.

CHAPTER 13

Heraclitus once mentioned in his notes that the world is "all in one," meaning that it is entirely interactive, with no actual distances inter-effective. However, the world is an endless myriad of interacting worlds, not just one, unless we believe in a man-made "solid" model in our imagination.

Is it possible to "objectively" measure the very speed of some light "out there?" No. Can we at least approximately measure our own human perception as the observer? Yes. According to our human perception of sight, the speed of light in a vacuum, commonly adopted as "a universal physical" constant, is "exactly equal" to 299,792,458 m/s. This statement is commonly understood incorrectly as being based on our ever-interactive human sensations through our relations with the entire world.

An imaginative idea and still naive belief that one appears as "a measure of all things" based on the privilege of being a human being, is only sarcastically expressed by the ancient philosopher Protagoras, the classical teacher on the immeasurable *unavoidable limitations* within the conditions of Flux where we exist. This form of "exact measuring" is only revealing how a "knowledgeable" man can become a grotesque of his pride of ignorance.

Is there "objectivity" in our measurements? However, if the sun is so "far away," why does our skin burn so easily?

When the world "wholeness" implies as "a fixed wholeness" within the powers of instant and continuous change, where nothing may truly be perfectly fixed or balanced, we shall begin our learning from within our own minds.

In any case, we are not born with blank minds. We as living beings are granted the faculty to sense our realities, whether we learn or just fantasize.

To begin to observe our own mind's deeply intuitive and vital *process of perceiving* based on our instant and unstoppable interactions within and without is a grand invitation to take a small step into a breathtaking future of fundamental findings about the nature of ourselves, similar to all living beings we may perceive.

Whether we punish ourselves with poor, boring, and monotonous, or even ugly mental productions, or we work happily to find creative ways to build and master peaceful and harmonious compositions to live in, both "physical," and mental, we have the freedom to choose our ways.

However, *there is no true FREEDOM of any sort without RESPONSIBILITY.* ***Freedom minus Responsibility equals Madness.***

Thus, we can explore our perceptions in unprecedented ways. Revealing our primordial mind's art, sound recordings, and animation studios, all in one living ephemeral chamber of the mind, we learn about our existence firsthand.

Creativity is rooted in every form of life for the sake of its own life and continuity through its unrepeatable unique transformations or living coexistence within inexhaustible powers of the worlds of flux.

The most effective learning method that is based on *Comparison* is leading us to *true cure* for the infectious idealism of false "objectivity."

To prevent further retardation of our intuitive intellect we still have to use our gadgets as less as possible. Nevertheless we need smart technology when we still cannot manage well on our own in cases of disasters. Some mass production of supplies can be urgently needed by many people or animals to be rescued.

Histories of philosophy and the sciences sometimes mention perceptions without even showing any curiosity about *why* we must perceive at all and *how we are able to perceive*. Therefore, our understanding of *the process* of constantly perceiving living minds is mainly ignored.

What is the mind. where it resides, and how it is getting empowered by the vital ephemeral energies to exist, cure and develop itself ?

As we, human beings, see ourselves, today, it is very hard to imagine that we may quickly turn into truly graceful, powerful and wise creatures.

No plastic surgeries trimming our physical bodies and faces may camouflage our nature. Your mind is your own nature.

Your mind can grow and heal your bodily composition from birth. The gate to the miracles is forever open. If we see our future existence away from our ridiculously primitive crutches of robotic machines imitating the world we would begin to break through the thick walls of millennia old mentalities and actions within established habits of our thinking. Inexhaustibly creative Nature is our ultimate school we still have never graduated. We may evolve not through childish imitation of things we cannot truly know but by discovering wisdom of coexistence with the living worlds.

Technology cannot choose in cases whether it shall help or demolish. Artificial technology cannot compensate for great human ignorance and AI tools cannot independently process thoughts. The great revision of our knowledge and actions is unavoidable for the sake of our very existence.

The mind is a little creator after its parental Spirit for the sake of vitality and evolution.

"ON BLESSED BLINDNESS," by V. Nova

... but if blindness of illusions
disappeared and everyone
could see
Every mind's Kingdom as is,
Feel every feeling and know every thought as one,
Misunderstandings could melt down forever.

Seeds of doubt and blame of others
could stop growing.

No fights, wars, intrigues, hate, no players or
pretending. Alas, no illusions of beauty, seductive
unknowns, or guesses.

No wonder and no wisdom—
all truths are clear for each mind and for all.

No thrill to admire, no one to thank,
No need to explain, to talk, to act, to scream.

No artist to paint.
No poet to sing.

If my peculiar human senses
cannot give me the world,
God bless my blindness,
the soil for my garden of dreams.

How little I can see with my eyes!
How endlessly I can see and create without them!

God bless my lonely mind in its sacred solitude, and
my only way

To know your world,
By building my own.

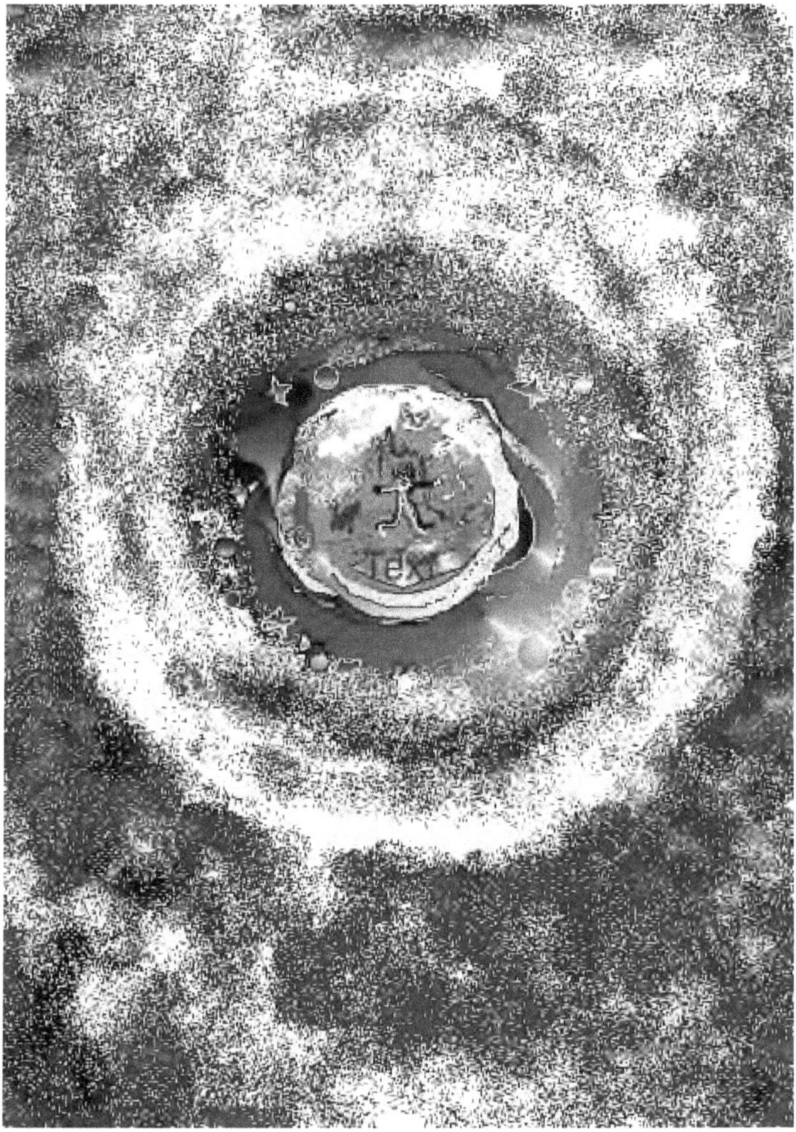

The Geography of a Living Mind

www.ingramcontent.com/pod-product-compliance
Lightning Source LLC
LaVergne TN
LVHW050917210926
848482LV00012B/479
9781806231607